Natural Su
l
Frank (

The beginner to intermediate technique book for learning and improving your surfing.
With 25 years experience teaching/coaching surfing privately and a professional career competing, I feel this book will give you a step forward in learning the art of surfing and get you to the next level with confidence. You will get both articulation and visual techniques I use daily and feel confident they will help you with your surfing and get you started on the right foot!

Frank Caronna owner/instructor Natural Surf Technique since 1989

Natural Surf Technique

ISBN-13: 978-0692253847
ISBN-10: 069225384X

Author- Frank Caronna
Editor- Debbie Waugh
Photography- David Stewart

Table of Contents

Preface: Why Surfing?

Surfing is like dancing on water. Wave after wave, the rhythm changes and the water becomes a surfer's creative canvas. Since the ocean is constantly in motion, no wave is ever the same making surfing one of the most difficult sports to learn. This versatility keeps surfers hooked and motivated to improve. Being a good surfer requires a combination of soul, patience, flow, and discipline.

Many people find surfing to be a life-changing experience. It defines who they are and is one of the things they love the most. I've ridden hundreds of waves and still love the sport as much as I did the day I caught my very first ride. With the right attitude and skill, anyone can surf for a lifetime.

Like anything worthwhile, surfing has its risks. That's why it's critical to minimize those risks with proper surf techniques, etiquette, and wave knowledge. Surfing smart means reaching a point where you can calculate the risks and paddle into bigger waves with confidence.

Even if you live far from the ocean and can't spend a lot of time in the water, you can still improve your skills by "couch surfing" and watching videos of some of the world's best surfers. I still watch my surf mentor, Tom Curren, a man who even championship surfer, Kelly Slater, considers a "master" of surfing.

When watching surf videos, study the way the pros paddle, how their hands push off of the board, and the flow they have when they're in the wave. Examine their form – from compression to extension – and the way they move their feet and turn the board in the wave. Pay close attention to the execution of bottom turns and how a turn can set up the rest of the ride. Watching surf videos can't replace actual surfing, but memorizing moves helps when you finally reach the water.

This book draws on more than 20 years of experience as a surf instructor and provides techniques to start surfing the safest, fastest way. Even if you're an experienced surfer, this book offers great reminders and helps hone in on things you may never have learned and want to improve.

In the following chapters, I'll cover a number of techniques for beginning and intermediate surfers. Certain topics are addressed repeatedly so you won't need to constantly refer back to previous chapters. I believe a combination of knowledge, practice, conditioning, confidence and risk leads the way to becoming a successful surfer.

Surfers know one good wave can make their whole day. This book will help you catch waves that will make your day, and your days for years to come.

Good luck with your surfing!
-- *Frank Caronna*
   Owner, Natural Surf Technique

Introduction: My Story

I was introduced to the ocean when I was only 7-years old, but it would take another four years before I finally started surfing.

Every summer, my father, brother and I would ride the boat to Catalina Island to go deep-sea fishing. We'd spend hours on the ocean, trolling for marlin or swordfish. I'd climb up to the Tuna Tower (the very highest part of the boat used to spot marlin). Standing up there I learned how to read the ocean's conditions and swells. I developed my balance, using my knees to adjust to the rolling waves. I knew if I didn't, I'd risk falling from the tower, a drop straight down of about 40-feet. I also noticed the winds and how they'd change. Most of the time in Southern California, the winds are calm in the morning and pick up in the afternoon, making the sea choppy. Long before I thought about riding a wave, my early fishing trips taught me plenty about the ocean.

When I was 10, my friends introduced me to body boarding. I absolutely loved the feeling of being in the water. Riding waves became the only thing I enjoyed more than fishing. Using what I'd learned about the ocean, I was catching the waves faster than my friends. Being small, I started on small waves, but slowly, and with practice, my confidence grew and started trying to ride bigger waves. In those days, body boards didn't have leashes so if you fell you would have to swim in to get it.

Swimming all the way in to shore to retrieve my board was exhausting and made me upset. So, I learned to hold onto my board and anticipate when larger waves were coming. Learning patience and timing the hard way paid off when I finally started surfing.

At the end of summer, we went camping with our friends and family in Carlsbad. The waves were good, but breaking far from shore. I saw a lot of surfers catching waves and thought it looked like a lot of fun. I studied them a long time. I only had a body board. I couldn't surf, could I?

Many, many failed attempts and days later, I finally stood up on my body board. The ride didn't last long or go very far, but I was up! Now I wanted to learn to surf. The only problem was, in finding my own way up on the body board, I'd developed bad habits no surfer wants.

When we returned home, the first thing I asked my mom for was a surfboard so I could learn to surf. She wasn't too thrilled as she thought surfing was dangerous. Every weekend when we'd go to the beach, I'd ask again. At the time, I had no idea she really couldn't afford to buy me a surfboard.

So, I began asking any surfer I saw if I could ride their board, but no one wanted to take a risk loaning their prized possession to such a little kid.

One weekend my friend's older brother came to the beach with his surfboard. When I asked if I could borrow his board, he said, "no way, you might ding it." I told him, "I bet I can stand up on my very first wave. If I don't, I'll never bother you for your board again." He agreed to the deal and before he could change his mind, I grabbed his board and headed for the water.

My first thought was, "Wow. Where do I lay on this thing? It's so much bigger than my body board." Just paddling in the white wash (foamy, already broken waves) was difficult. My little 4'10" frame was trying to hold on to a 7' surfboard and getting tossed around. I decided it was easier to pick up the board and turn it toward the beach rather than trying to lie on it first and then turning it around in the water.

Since I knew my friend's brother was giving me only one chance, I had to be balanced. Remembering the Tuna Tower sat in the middle of the fishing boat, I decided that's where I should be too: in the middle of the board.

Working up my courage, I turned the board toward the beach, laid flat in the middle of the board and as the white wash pushed me, I held on as tight as I possibly could and right before I reached the shore, I stood up!

It wasn't a very long ride, but my friend's brother was so happy and impressed, he let me keep surfing on his board.

I got more comfortable and in spite of the bad habits I'd developed, rode plenty of waves and had countless wipeouts. Leaving the beach that day I was addicted and even more determined to talk my mom into buying me a surfboard!

Summer came and went without a surfboard of my own. I was so heartbroken. I wouldn't even go body boarding. For a month, my friends would beg me to join them at the beach, but being a very stubborn 10 year-old, I refused to go unless I got a surfboard. Another month passed, school started, and I lost hope.

One day, my mom said she saw someone down the street was selling a used surfboard and asked if I wanted to take a look. Before she could even finish the sentence, I was in the car and ready to go! When I saw the board, I immediately wanted it, but the price was still too high. My mom said she was sorry she couldn't afford it and I started to cry. The only consolation I had was I knew she'd finally warmed up to the idea of me surfing.

Another week passed and I came home after hanging out at the mall with my friends. It was my birthday and they had taken me out for ice cream. When I walked in, my mom asked if I'd grab something for her from the garage. As I walked into the garage, directly in front of me was the surfboard we'd seen earlier wrapped in a big bow with a sign reading, "Happy 11th Birthday, Frankie!"

I was so happy! I came running in, gave my mom the biggest hug, and said, "Thank you, mommy, I love it!" I held my arms out wide and told her, "And I love you this much more!"

The board wasn't new. Actually, it was pretty beat up. But that 6'6" Dewey Weber with a green deck (top) and fuchsia rails (sides) and bottom was all mine! It didn't have any wax on it, so I called around to find a place that carried wax.

When we got to the beach around 8:30 a.m. the next morning, my mom took me to the surf shop to buy wax, but it didn't open until 10 a.m. So we waited. And we waited. Finally, the clerk showed up, hair wet and still half in his wetsuit apologizing for being late because "the waves were really good!" I realized, "Wow, that is so cool. When you surf, you can be late to work or even to school!" I found out later life didn't work that way, but at the time, it seemed to make perfect sense.

We asked for wax and he handed us a bar of Mr. Zog's Sex Wax. My mom was shocked and asked him, "Uh, what is this?" She didn't care for the name, so she made me take the plastic wrapper off the wax and carry it the bag instead. It didn't matter. I had my wax, I had my board, and I was heading to the beach!

On the sand, I applied more wax, doing it the way the surf shop clerk showed me, wrapped the leash around my ankle and got in the water.

I still remember how hard it was to paddle and keep my balance. Just as I had on my friend's brother's board, I caught white wash the entire time. There were some rides, but mostly I wiped out and my board went flipping around. Luckily, I didn't get hit (at least not that day).

When we finally left the beach my mom could see by the look in my eyes I'd be surfing for a long time. Wanting to make me happy, she also knew she'd be spending a lot more time at the beach.

Catching your first wave can change your life.

I know, because at just 11-years old, it changed mine.

Chapter 1

Gear-ing Up: How to Choose the Right Surfboard

In skateboarding or snowboarding everyone learns on similar size boards. Surfing is different. Your equipment has to float and the surface you're learning on is in constant motion. Boards must be chosen based on a surfer's height, weight, and prior water experience. Proper conditioning for surfing requires hours of time spent in the water. Like any sport, the more you go, the better you'll get, but having the proper board will improve the speed at which you learn. If you want to ride a shortboard, you should expect to surf daily. Typically, kids on summer break who surf every day move from a longboard to a shortboard in less than 3 months. Adults who can only surf a couple of times per week generally take longer.

SIZES AND SHAPES

Longboards

Longboards measure between 9 feet or more in length. They typically have either 1 or 3 fins and a round nose. The thickness of a longboard depends on the surfer's weight, height, and surfing experience. Beginners typically start on a longboard that's at least 2 to 3 feet longer than *their height to increase their paddling speed and make balancing easier. Many experienced surfers prefer longboards and ride them in all surf conditions, especially in small or mushy (less powerful) waves where they can master a variety of stylish tricks.*

Funboards
Funboards measure between 7 to 9 feet in length and are shaped like a longboard. Funboards are best with 3 fins and are great for beginning or intermediate surfers who want to learn how to turn in the face of a wave. They are typically thicker for increased paddling speed and perfect for surfers working their way down from a longboard to a shortboard.

Shortboards
Shortboards range from 5 feet to over 6 feet depending on the surfer's height and weight. Shortboards can have 1 to 5 fins and should be ridden by experienced surfers who know how to paddle correctly and catch waves. Shortboards require more strength to paddle. Timing and condition are also crucial. Beginning surfers who switch too quickly to shortboards can develop bad techniques and style, resulting in longer learning times. Most people don't realize even the pros started out on bigger boards.

DESIGNS AND FINS
Surfboards are made from a variety of materials ranging from styrofoam to epoxy. Designs are

based upon the way a surfer and the board moves across the waves. The slightest changes in the design can make huge differences in the way the board performs. Some surfboards are designed by computers, but most are created by shapers, talented artists who craft boards by hand.

Length
The length of a surfboard is measured underneath from nose to tail.

Rocker

*Rocker refers to the curve that runs from nose to tail. This curvature helps the board turn in the wave. The greater
the rocker, the tighter the turn a surfboard can make. However, too much rocker will cause the surfboard to slow down and push water. For beginners and the majority of surfers, an average amount of rocker is best.*

Nose
The nose of a surfboard is the front end of the board. The shape of the nose – how round or how pointed – determines how a surfboard paddles and turns.

Rails

Rails form the sides or outline of the surfboard and come in different thicknesses. Thin rails make it easy to apply pressure and set the edge of the board in a wave. Rails that are too thin decrease buoyancy and are better for experienced surfers who can generate speed and have greater control.

Edges

The bottom of the rail is called the edge. A hard edge is usually found in the tail and grows softer toward the nose of the surfboard. Edges play an important role in the way a board rides across a wave. Most surfers prefer a very sharp edge along the back 15-inches of the tail that tapers to round through the middle and nose of the board. If a surfboard is catching its rail when riding the face of a wave, it might be the edge near the front foot is too sharp. A softer front foot edge allows the board to roll through the water easily. Sharper rails work well in glassy conditions and better waves, but aren't ideal for all-around surfing (unless you have a few different boards to choose from). Ultimately, ride what feels good and find out how to make it work in different conditions. I ride my 5'10" tri fin with a squash tail 80 percent of the time and if the waves have over 6-foot faces, I'll ride anything from a 6'0" to a 7'0" depending upon the type of wave. I even have fun riding a longboard when the waves are small.

Fins

What's the difference between 1, 2, or 3 fins on a surfboard? That's easy. A single fin surfboard is harder to turn, but offers greater stability for beginners. Twin fins (2 fins) or tri fins (3 fins) on a shortboard turn easier, generate speed, and have tighter turning radiuses. Most longboards have one to three fin set-ups and either work well for a beginning surfer. Learning to surf is mostly about foot placement, but different fin setups can help you turn more effectively in certain waves and ocean conditions. Fin shapes range from foil (deeply curved) to lower amounts of curve. They're inspired by fish fins and similar to the rudder on a boat, stabilizing the surfer so the board won't slide out while riding a wave. Boards without fins are nearly impossible to ride. Fins change the way a board turns, gains speed, and flows—just like they help fish swim and dolphins hunt!

Tails

The design of the tail—like everything else—helps the way a board turns and trims across a wave. Beginner surfers rarely notice a difference in tail designs until they've performed advanced tricks on the face of the wave like cutbacks, off the lips, carves, and aerials.
Pintails *come to a point at the tail of the board. Pintails are usually better in steeper waves or on longboards. They allow for smooth turns without a sliding effect. Most surfers in Hawaii ride pintails on bigger, steeper days because they're perfect for tube riding. Pintails allow the fins to be set closer together so the board is stiffer with less lift. Pintails hold in a wave better than other tail designs.*
Squash/Square tails *are wider and flatter. They allow for easier flow and rail-to-rail work. Squash*

tails provide better release when turning off the top of waves and are great for surfers learning new tricks. The wider shape generates more lift in the tail so it is easier to generate speed and make tight radius turns. This tail design is the most common and is popular on shortboards and funboards.

Swallowtails are accurately named with a fork-like look and two points like a swallow's tail. Similar to a squash tail, the shape changes the way the board flows and turns. Some surfers prefer swallowtails, but I recommend learning to ride waves effectively before experimenting with different tail designs.

WETSUITS AND STAYING WARM

Full suits are wetsuits that cover your entire body except your hands, feet and head. Wetsuits come in different thicknesses based upon the water and air temperature where you're surfing. Fit is key as your wetsuit should be snug and fit tightly like a sock or a glove. If your wetsuit is too big, water will flush in and out and your body temperature will drop. Ideally, a wetsuit should allow only in a thin layer of water which warms to your body temperature and helps keep you warm. When you're shopping for a wetsuit, ask the surf shop for advice and try on a number of different brands until you find one that works with your body type.

Short-sleeve full suits are designed like full suits, but have short sleeves and are made for slightly warmer 60-degree water and air temperatures.

Spring suits have short legs and short sleeves, are slightly thinner and designed for warmer 66 to 70-degree water and air temperatures. Similar to a full suit, the fit should be comfortable but snug.

Booties and hats are accessories used to cover your feet and head in colder 50-degree water and air temperatures. Booties are worn like shoes and should fit snugly with your toes touching. If your toes don't touch, cold water can enter the bootie and make your feet feel cold or slosh around when you're riding a wave. For example, I typically wear a size 9 shoe, but size 8 booties. Booties can also be worn to protect your feet whenever you're surfing in a spot with rocks, a reef, or even stingrays.

Chapter 2

Sea Sense: The Importance of Wind, Waves & Breaks

Changing Ocean Conditions

The most important things to consider when you're about to surf are the tides and wind conditions.

Tides

Ocean tides change constantly. Some days have large tide swings and others minimal. Tides are important because they affect how waves break. Lower tides work better in some spots, while higher tides work better in others. If you're surfing a reef break or a spot that's rocky, you'll need to know if the tide is coming in or going out and the heights. When the tide goes out, the water will become shallow creating steeper waves. Incoming tides bring additional swell but can lack steepness. Ultimately, it all depends on the break you're surfing.

Generally, beach breaks work best on medium to high tides unless the direction of the swell direction is at a perfect angle for the beach, sand bars, or sand banks. Sand bars are areas on the ocean floor that go from deep to shallow within yards and improve wave shape. The ocean floor at most beach breaks is constantly changing depending on the tides and wave shapes.

Before you go surfing, always check the conditions and know whether the tides are rising or falling. I'll usually watch the waves from shore for 10 minutes to determine where the best shape is and whether the tides are coming up or going down.

Wind

Wind angles have an enormous effect on waves and how they break. Offshore winds blow from land toward the ocean and because they keep wave faces smooth, are usually the most favorable for surfers. In the morning, the wind can be calm or offshore, but in the afternoon if often switches onshore creating choppy, mixed up surf. Strong onshore winds make it hard for anyone but expert watermen and experienced surfers to judge (or enjoy) the waves.

Due to their shapes, point breaks and jetties can have clean wave faces even during strong wind conditions. Winds typically die down immediately before sunset creating a condition known as "evening glass off." The lack of wind during this time period creates clean, smooth wave faces and great surf sessions.

Wind is relative to where you live and where you surf. Hawaii can be cleaner and have better surf in the afternoon unlike many other places around the globe.

Waves

Some surf breaks are great for all levels while others are for experienced surfers only. Always look for a break with waves where you can enjoy longer, better rides. At beach breaks, you'll find both waves that break to the left and the right (lefts and rights). Waves at point breaks or reef breaks typically go in one direction.

Most surf breaks are affected by tide height, wave height, and swell direction. Beach breaks are usually best when the swell direction comes from two different angles, causing the waves to peak (have a distinguished left or right angle). Sometimes waves will break better in one direction than another, but it all depends on the factors mentioned previously. In summer, waves come primarily from the south, meaning waves with a left angle will have better shape. Be aware strong south-to-north currents can also occur. In winter, the reverse is true, and waves with a right angle have better shape. Abstractions such as piers, islands or jetties, can also alter wave conditions.

Always pay close attention to how the waves and currents are behaving before paddling out. Surf forecast sites such as surfline.com or swellmagnet.com offer forecasts and live cams so you can see the conditions before you reach the beach.

The best and longest waves in California are found at point breaks, such as Malibu or Rincon. These two popular right point breaks can be very crowded with experienced surfers and are not recommended for surfers who haven't mastered surf conditioning, confidence, or etiquette.

"Locals," or people who have surfed the same location for many years and are often protective of overcrowding, frequent the majority of surf spots. It's important to respect local surfers and if you're still learning, surf away from them. This allows everyone the opportunity to enjoy the waves—the locals won't be worried about inexperienced surfers getting in their way and beginners have room to learn and catch their own waves. When you're a beginning or intermediate surfer, I always recommend surfing away from the crowd. Even if it seems like the waves are better where they are, there's no reason to join the crowd and compete with more aggressive, experienced surfers until you're ready.

Chapter 3

Getting Your Feet Wet: A Quick Start

Know Before You Go

Before you paddle out for the very first time, you
need to know how to choose the proper equipment
and recognize a variety of ocean conditions.

Choosing a Surfboard

If you're a beginner, choose a surfboard a
minimum of 2-feet taller than your height, keeping
your weight, flexibility, and prior ocean experience
in mind. For example, if you are 6-feet tall, in great
physical shape, and with a fair amount of
experience in the ocean, you'll do well learning on
an 8-foot or longer surfboard.

Bigger boards tend to paddle easier and move
slower in the water, providing you with more time
to perfect your technique, increase your paddling
speed, and gain your balance – all very valuable
when you're learning. If you find your technique
and wave-catching abilities are already suffering on
a longer board, going shorter will only make things
worse.

As you improve, you can gradually decrease your
board size (typically moving down 6-inches at a
time).

When to Go

Choose a day with small waves, usually 1- to 2-feet in height, or in the whitewash (foam created after the wave has broken) until your confidence and ocean knowledge have improved.

Gain Your Footing

Surfers are always either "regular" footed or "goofy" footed. Regular-footed surfers stand on the board with their left foot forward and use their right foot to steer the back of the board. Goofy-footed surfers have the opposite stance. To determine your stance, try having someone stand behind you and give you a gentle push forward. Pay attention to which foot you automatically step forward with first. Or, imagine doing a cartwheel and how you would turn your feet.

Beach Yourself

Place the surfboard on the beach with the fins down and the nose (front) pointing toward the ocean. Locate the middle of the board and if possible, draw a wax line across the middle of the board, which is the approximately the boards balancing spot and then do the same for an eye line in 2nd photo. Lay on the board with your chest resting slightly ahead of this middle point. One key thing to remember is soft boards are easier to practice the technique of getting to your feet. Hard boards are typically covered with a coat of wax, preventing your feet and body from sliding easily.

A board with wax on it will be easier to practice the slide up once it's wet or you are in in the ocean surfing. If you only have a hard board with wax, I recommend making sure it is wet on the surface so you don't stick as much and causing you to possibly stick and trip.

Here I mark the board with wax for two visual spots-1) The middle of the board where my sternum needs to be or just below depending on a person body type and 2) My eye line also helps me avoid being too far up.

From here you want to lift your head up and pull your shoulders together to create a slight arch in your back as shown in the next couple photos. This allows you to see better and control the *nose* of the board. Remember to keep your feet low and close together (not hanging off the sides of the board). You may even want to cross your feet, so you have one less thing to remember. The next photo shows hand position for performing the slide technique. Notice the heal of my palm is at the center of the board with elbows in for strength and control for pushing up, while my knees and feet are together with toes slightly touching the board. The key is to lift your upper body up and slide forward off the knees and tips of your toes with your front foot getting to middle of the board between your hands. You will want to practice this move at home on hard wood floor or tile floor to get it down and perfect the slide. From here its about rotating your lower body with front foot leading and get your feet to be perpendicular when you are standing. Usually front foot is on a slight more angle with back foot horizontal as its easier to balance and control the boards turning ability. The best stance that will help with gaining speed and flow is about shoulder width apart, while stepping back with the back foot to the tail will help with the boards turning ability once you start learning to turn.

Paddle Practice

Paddling has 3 distinct speeds. First Speed is a "doggie paddle," usually about eight strokes to start moving through the water and is done with your head and chest slightly up so you can see easier. Second Speed involves longer and deeper strokes and lowering your head slightly. Finally, Third Speed occurs by dropping your chest and chin low to the board, reaching even further, and keeping your eyes on the ocean (not on the board).

In this photo I am watching the bigger side of wave over my shoulder till it reaches the tail of the board. By doing this I can see the wave better and also see if another surfer is on the wave riding or not.

*In the second photo I am looking ahead or in the
direction I want to ride. In the third photo I have
taken a deep breath and then exhaling as I am
dropping my chin while reaching further so that I
can gain planning speed and catch the wave easier.
Remember to keep your knees and feet together as
you paddle to control tail lift and makes going to
your feet easier with the slide up technique.*

Perfecting the timing of lowering your chin to the board and keeping the nose from dipping underwater is important. (That's why keeping your feet close together is crucial and will help control tail lift.) If you lower your chin before the wave starts to push you, the nose will go underwater a majority of the time and you'll fall down the front of the wave, also known as "pearling."

If you find the nose of the board is constantly going underwater as you're paddling, check to ensure your chest is resting in the right position just in front of the middle of the board (adjust if necessary) and that your feet are together.

FOR THE LITTLE ONES/KIDS:

For smaller kids, roughly ages 5 to 10 years, place them slightly further back on larger boards, with their chests approximately 1-inch below the middle. I always recommend larger boards for beginners, even if it's a funboard or longboard, but if your kids are learning on a small, 5-foot foam board, use the same paddle position and techniques as for an adult.

It's important to remember kids will need to be reminded frequently about technique, including keeping their feet together, hands close to the body, heels of the palms even with their sternum, etc. Since they weigh less, it is also harder for them to control the tail of the board. Try pushing the tail down as the wave begins to lift them. It will keep the nose from going under (pearling) and keep them from falling and getting discouraged.

The Slide Up

There's a technique everyone can use to stand up on a surfboard: **The Slide Up. The Slide Up is a technique that I designed to help coordinate a beginning surfers body till the surfer develops more strength and better surf knowledge. The Slide Up will evolve into the pop up which is what you see the better surfers and pros use.**

The best board to practice the slide up on is a soft board as the wax on a hard board will cause your body to stick. Once a waxed board is in the water, than the technique will be easier to apply and you wont stick as much. If you can't make it to the beach, practice your Slide Up on a tile or wood floor as seen in the first few photos with few more verbal details.

Lay on the board in the correct position (chest just ahead of the middle point). Bend your elbows and place your hands flat on the board slightly below chest level with the heels of your palms flat on the middle of the board. This will help control your balance as you lift to your feet. Do not grab the rails (side edges of the surfboard).

With your hands in this position, lift your upper body then pull your hips forward while sliding your feet through. (See Previous Photos.) Never allow the tips of your toes to leave your board during the Slide Up. Always try and focus on pulling your front knee into your chest where the middle of board is.

Aim to finish this move with your feet shoulder-width apart, the front foot in the middle of the board between your hands, and the back foot approximately 2 feet behind. This will improve your flow when you begin pumping to gain speed on waves. Eventually you will learn to step back on the tail of the board to turn better and easier while riding.

In the water, once you start catching waves you will see this technique will really help you stay down the middle of the board, while jumping can have a tendency to many times off center your feet which will take away from good foot placement and balance.. As you improve you will see that this technique will really help transition into smaller boards.

I remember a few times growing up watching from the pier my favorite pro surfers like Tom Curren and Mark Richards at the OP Pro contest in Huntington Beach and what I noticed was how easy they went from paddling into the wave to getting to their feet. I noticed mostly that they kept their lower body close to the board as they went to their feet.

I practice daily to improve and make it part of my repertoire as well, but when you can't surf everyday you need to find a way to continue practicing and is one of the key things I share with my students.

For larger surfers (who have more to lift) the Slide Up may take some time to perfect. I recommend practicing at home on a hardwood or tile floor as described above since it makes sliding easier.

Practicing the Slide Up until it feels natural will help you get you to your feet quicker and catch your footing faster. Balance will come naturally when your feet are flat on the board and your body is upright.

Remember to pull your body, and not the board, forward. If you push the board forward you'll stand up too far back on the tail (end) of the board and either lose your balance or miss the wave completely. Too wide a stance will also hinder your flow, so as you slide keep both feet together until the last possible moment.

Ocean Conditions:

Learning to watch the surf before paddling out is always wise.
Watch and notice where the waves are breaking. Are there bigger sets occasionally? What are the currents doing?

When I started surfing, I didn't have an instructor (or this book!) so I learned by trial and error. This is one reason why I stress the importance of being thoroughly aware of what's happening in the ocean before you paddle out.

I remember a day when the waves looked really fun. My friend and I were excited to get in the water. Only a few other surfers were out and we didn't spend a lot of time assessing the conditions. It looked like it would take a decent amount of paddling to reach where they were sitting, patiently waiting for something.

My friend and I started paddling out. About half way, we noticed a big set rising up and coming our way with maybe 6- to 8-foot wave faces. We started paddling faster. The waves kept growing. We knew we were looking at the set waves.

The first wave broke right before we reached it and I decided to try to duck dive. I was nearly able to hold on, but the wave was too powerful. The board was ripped out of my grasp. My friend bailed his board, the wave caught it, and his leash snapped. When we popped back up, we realized his board had hit another surfer on the arm, leaving him bruised.

By now, my friend's board was caught in the current and heading toward shore. But he was in bigger trouble than his board. The ocean's powerful swell was washing him toward the rocks and he was very scared. Luckily, we got through it but my friend was scraped up pretty badly.

If we taken the time to notice the conditions we would have chose another spot or waited for the right time to paddle out.

Chapter 4

Standing: Practicing in the whitewash and learning to build your confidence.

Before you paddle out into deeper water, practice in the whitewash (foam where the wave has already broken) to get a better feel for your board and work on your technique and balance.

Choose a beach break and pick a spot away from crowds of surfers or swimmers. You'll be learning the basics of paddling and getting to your feet.

My clients usually have the best luck in smaller, less strenuous waves. Unfortunately, the ocean doesn't always cooperate so you may have to practice at times in rougher conditions.

First

For your first session, pick a day when the tides are low or medium. This will allow you to walk your board out to waist deep water and save your arm strength for catching the whitewash/foam and learning to go up to your feet. Conditioning will come with practice.

Second

Once you have walked out approximately 2/3 of the way to where the waves are breaking, turn your

board directly toward beach and stand next to it,
keeping an eye on any oncoming wave

Third

To lie on the board, grab the rails at the center of
your board as seen in photo above and slide on to
the board coming up from either side of the tail
area (try to do this smoothly, sliding not jumping
onto the board). Keep your legs and feet close
together and raise your head as high as possible
when you start to paddle. Being in the correct spot
with your chest slightly in front of the middle of
your board as previously mentioned is very
important at this time and why using visual marks
are helpful when you first learn.

Fourth

After the wave breaks, start paddling for the whitewash that's rolling your way and keep watching over your shoulder as seen in the photo above. When you feel the whitewash push the tail of the surfboard, drop your chin, look toward the beach, exhale, and take a few longer, stronger paddles. If you are slightly angled and your board is not directed straight at the beach, the whitewash may catch one of the rails and cause you to flip over or miss the wave. Once you learn to control the board better with lots of practice, you can start learning to paddle on a slight angle to help project you in a given direction while setting the inside edge or the edge closest to the wave or whitewash/foam.

Fifth

Once you've caught the wave and its momentum is pushing you, use everything you've learned. With your body balanced and your feet together, bring your hands to rest close to your body with palms down near the middle of the board as seen in next photo(do not grab the rails). From here, do exactly what you learned on the beach. Do not worry about balancing, just focus on coming to your feet in one smooth motion. Balance will come after your feet are flat and standing on the board.

Notice that my front knee comes down the middle of the board staying inside my arms. This is important as you will have a hard time getting to your feet properly if the front knee goes outside the arm to get up. From here is when you twist just your lower body to get your feet to turn into position, which will give you better balance and control.

Then once you are up, keep your weight favoring over the front foot as shown in the photo above. To turn you would shift your weigh to the back leg while keep your upper body forward still. Shifting the weight to the back foot will also keep the nose from going under on steeper drops during the drop or cut, but then goes back over the front foot to gain balance and momentum when needed.

Sixth

Lift your upper body and in one motion pull your lower body forward and slide your feet through. Do not hesitate or attempt to move slowly, it will only make you feel unstable and you'll lose control. As you come up, twist the lower body only, leading with the front foot. Keep your upper body, arms, and shoulders almost perpendicular to board and your hands up and out at shoulder level. Place your arms on about a 45-degree angle for balance and try and keep more weight on your front foot. Practice keeping your balance while riding the whitewash and keep your knees bent and flexible, not extended or locked.

Seventh

If your balance is improving and you're getting to your feet consistently, try shifting your weight back slightly and turning in one direction. This may take time and practice for your body to learn. (Tip: if you look where you're headed, your body will eventually follow.) Practice riding waves in one direction until it feels comfortable and then switch to ride the other way. The wave's shape will determine whether you'll go left or right. Always watch for other surfers and follow proper surf etiquette. Turning is done by applying pressure on the rail or side of the board. If you want to go right, then the right rail needs to have more pressure and sink it gradually under water while your weight is shifted back to the back foot. Too much pressure over the front foot can make the nose or rail catch for beginners. Practice, you will get it!

Eighth

After you've gotten comfortable riding the whitewash, you can begin to understand compression and extension, where flow, style, and speed are born. Get as low as you can, keeping your weight on the instep of your back foot and lift and extend your entire body up nearly all the way, then compress again(this is called pumping the board for speed). Think about it like doing squats with weights on your shoulders, but favoring the instep on your back foot. Practice this slowly and evenly until you can maintain control and balance. Surfing with good flow is important and your compression and extension will change with every wave. Surfers with the best style usually have their weight on their instep and knees closer together while the feet maintain shoulder width apart or wider for turning ability. Trying this first on land or on a skateboard helps many of my students get a better feel for compression and extension.

Ninth

When you start feeling comfortable with all of these things, try turning your board on a wave. Take your back foot and step further back on the tail. If you try to turn without stepping back or merely shifting your hips, you'll probably catch your rail and fall. Turning gets the nose of the board set and lifted.

Don't worry too much when you're first starting, as eventually instincts will take over.

Tenth

After plenty of practice in the whitewash or on small waves, you'll have the confidence you need to surf better waves. It may take a few months of practice to truly feel comfortable. Surfing like any sport is all about an individual's natural ability combined with practice. Using what you've learned will help you catch waves on small days and on big wave days, give you things to work on in the whitewash.

Chapter 5

Paddling: Getting in the Wave

Having been a surf instructor for 25 years, I've learned the best way to help beginner and intermediate surfers improve their surfing abilities by following a few techniques.

Laying on the Board

As mentioned, start with a visual spot by drawing a line in the wax across the very middle of your board. This will help you find your balancing point on the surfboard. People also have a balancing point, and for most surfers it's their sternum. When lying on the board, place your sternum slightly in front of the middle line. Keep your legs and feet together to control the tempo of the tail. You don't want it moving up too high while you're paddling. If your feet slip off the sides of the board to help you balance, you'll reduce your paddling speed, be more likely to pearl (fall down the nose of the board), and lose the ability to get on your feet with good technique. If keeping your feet together feels awkward, try crossing your feet when you paddle and going out on a small day, practicing until it starts to feel natural.

Lift Off

To control your board properly as you paddle, arch your lower back and lift your upper body off the board. This will help you see the ocean and waves easier. Everyone has different degrees of flexibility and core strength, so don't strain yourself, simply do your best and work on improving.

Lead with Your Fingertips

As you paddle, remember you want to keep control of the board with proper body positioning. The key is to glide over the water. Keeping your head and shoulders up will help you see the ocean and waves. Lowering your head will help you plane and paddle faster. Be sure the nose of your board stays above the water. From there, keep your hands close to the rails (sides of the board) as you paddle and lead with your fingertips followed by your palms. Do not slap the water. Think of your fingertips entering the water like a diver, fast and smooth. If possible, try paddling so your hands push water under the board rather than dispersing water away from the board. Imagine creating a stream that flows under the board and toward the tail. This will help to improve your control and speed while paddling. Everyone is different, so try different techniques until you find what works best.

Keep Watching

Keep your eyes on the wave coming from behind you until it starts pushing you and your board, then turn your head toward the beach. Don't look down at the bottom of the wave or at your board. This will cause you to hesitate and lose your technique. When you're first learning, always catch a wave and go straight toward the beach until you gain your balance. Once you've mastered going straight and keeping your eyes up, try turning your head and looking in the direction you want to ride (either right or left, depending on the wave). As the wave starts to push you, look in the direction you want to go and picture your take off. Soon and with practice, you'll discover there are many different ways to create a route across the face of a wave.

Perfect Your Technique

Continue paddling with your head up, keeping an eye on the wave and any surfers who might be up and riding. The surfer closest to the curl has the right of way and you don't want to drop in, cutting off someone who is already on a wave. That's why looking over your shoulder is so important. To catch the wave, drop your chin low to the board, keep your legs and feet together, increase the speed and length of your strokes, and when you finally feel you have enough momentum to catch it, slide up quickly until you're standing and riding the wave!

Chapter 6

Catching & Riding Waves

*Now that you've had time to practice your Slide Up
on the beach and in the whitewash, it's time to
catch your first wave! There's nothing more
enjoyable (or memorable) than paddling into a
wave, getting up to your feet, keeping your balance,
and riding towards the shore or cutting across the
wave. Here's how to make that happen:*

Location, Location, Location

*Choose a day when the waves are small and gentle,
preferably just one- to two-feet in height, on a
medium tide, and in a spot that's not too crowded.
Crowds of other surfers will only distract you while
you're learning, so if you're surfing a beach break,
simply walk further down the beach and away from
the crowd before paddling out.*

Paddling Out

*On a day with small waves, paddling out isn't too
challenging, but it's important to keep a few things
in mind. Try to time your paddle out during a lull
between wave sets, so you'll easily make it out
before the waves start breaking. If you realize a
wave is going to break in front of you, you'll need to
"turtle roll" or turn your board upside down which
will allow the impact of the breaking wave to wash*

across the bottom of the board. If you are riding a shortboard you will need to learn how to duck dive, which is pushing the front end of the board under water and then with your back foot, you can step on the tail and push the tail under or use your knee to help. Duck diving is about getting deeper under the power of the white wash, the nose goes under first with the tail second. It takes practice and you don't need a wave to practice, just some paddling momentum then practicing the maneuver.

Turtle Rolling

To turtle roll, grab the rails (sides of the board) at chest to shoulder level tightly, lean to one side, and roll upside down keeping the nose of the board pointing directly into the wave. If the nose of the board is not completely straight and pointed at the incoming waves or is on a slight angle, there's a chance the wave will yank your board out of your hands and flip it over. You'll want to have turtle rolled (turned the board) completely before the wave reaches you. Once you feel the turbulence from the passing wave has ended, roll the board back over, slide up onto it, and continue paddling out. Since waves come in sets, you may have to repeat your turtle dive a few times before you make it past a set of breaking waves.

Notice in the sequence of photos my board is straight at the wave and I grab the rails close to the middle of the board and keep the board close to my body for balance, control and strength as mentioned.

The trick here is to try and roll back over quickly in case another wave is coming and should be practiced many times without going under a wave to get a better idea and build your confidence in the technique.

Keep Your Eye on the Ocean

Now you've made it past where the waves are breaking. What next? From here, you should watch the waves to determine where the majority of them are breaking. Always keep an eye out for oncoming waves and be ready to paddle out further if necessary as shown in the next photo. You should aim to sit a minimum of 15 to 20 feet (or double the length of your board) beyond where the waves are breaking. As you watch the waves, practice sitting on your board, keeping your hips slightly behind the middle of your board. You may also want to practice turning your board, holding one rail and using the other to help turn and also circling your feet can help some until the nose of the surfboard is facing the shore.

This photo shows how to sit and watch the wave as you turn to paddle and try and catch it. Notice I am sitting just behind the middle of the board with my hand on one rail and will use the other to help me turn the board. I also keep my upper body slightly forward for balance and control while the nose is sticking up slightly to allow easier turning. You need to practice this quite a bit out past the waves or can be done when the waves are flat to improve your technique of sitting and turning with control and balance.

Go With the Flow

When you feel comfortable sitting on your board and know where the waves are breaking, look for a wave you want to catch. Remember, you should be sitting approximately 15 to 20 feet from where the wave will break which means when you first notice a wave coming, start paddling before it is 15 to 20 feet from where you'll catch it. Think of it as splitting the difference. If a wave is going to break 20 feet from where you are, then start paddling when the wave is 20 feet away. Don't worry about paddling super fast. Simply stay comfortable and focus on your technique. Paddling speed will increase as you improve. Sometimes it's a great idea to go out further and learn how to paddle using the swell to gain momentum. Since you aren't worried about getting to your feet, you can relax and focus on perfecting your technique. Many of my students have tried practicing this way, and realized how much easier it is to catch a wave when they're relaxed, breathing, and focused on their technique rather than whether or not they caught the wave.

Timing is Everything

After you've mastered the technique and can consistently keep your balance in the whitewash, try paddling further out to catch a wave. Choose a day when the waves are small and select a spot away from the crowds. Pay attention to where the waves are breaking and paddle approximately 15 yards beyond this point.

Be sure to face the oncoming waves until you're ready to turn your board and paddle toward the beach. You'll be using the same techniques you practiced in the whitewash to stand up in waves.

At this point, it's better to get to your feet too soon rather than too late. If you find you're not catching waves, try taking a few more paddles before you Slide Up. Practicing in small waves will decrease your chances of getting hurt or hurting others. If the waves are too large, simply continue perfecting your technique in the whitewash.

Never push yourself to paddle out in waves if you're not ready. Usually, high tides with gentle waves are the easiest to learn in, but higher tides at beach breaks sometimes create steep shore breaks (rising up right before it hits the shore) and beginners should move past the shore break into deeper water. Always increase your confidence, knowledge, and skill before tackling bigger waves.

As you're paddling for a wave, keep your head up, and look over your shoulders like you did when you practiced in the white wash. Keep your paddling smooth. As you feel the momentum of the wave lift the tail of your board, take a deep breath, exhale, and drop your chin. Remember to keep your feet together and reach your paddling as far as possible taking four to six strokes until you feel yourself moving in time with the wave. As this moment, stop paddling, place your hands flat on the board and Slide Up. Paddling speed is important, but technique is crucial. You will learn to paddle faster as your conditioning improves. The key is to do everything quickly and as smoothly as possible, getting your front foot to the middle of the board, and your rear foot approximately shoulder width back. Make sure to pull your body straight forward, and don't twist too soon.

The wave here just gets to my tail of the board and I start looking forward at this moment and look for direction to ride. In this case the wave is bigger over my left shoulder so I will want to look and ride to the right. Its usually easier to catch the wave paddling straight ahead toward the beach and then the last few paddles set the edge a tiny bit in the direction you want to ride. Until you get more experienced and wave savvy this is the best and easiest way to start catching waves on your own.

In this photo I drop my chin low and now reach further while breathing out to let the wave take me easier and breathing out will help you catch waves with a faster glide. If you lower your chin too soon the nose can catch causing you to pearl/nosedive or miss the wave. It is very important to work on timing of this technique in smaller less steep waves. Always be sure to wait till the wave just starts pushing you before taking a deep breath and reaching further with your paddles, which will also help lower your chin get closer to the board.

As I go to my feet I am looking where I want to set my right rail/edge of the board to start cutting and ride the face of the wave.

Here I have set the edge and am riding right across the wave while watching the wave face to be inspired on what route to take to get the most out of the particular wave.

Take a Ride

Once you are on your feet and riding down the front of the wave, keep your weight over your front foot, then shift your weight onto your back foot to keep the nose of the board from pearling (going under). After you have made the drop, return your weight onto the front foot to keep your balance. Remember, the front half of your board has no weight on it, so keeping your weight at the center or on the front foot will help maintain your balance after you made the drop. If you keep your weight on the back foot, the wave can push it out from under you and you will probably fall off.

Try, Try Again

Catching waves with the right mix of timing and skill takes practice and patience. If you get on your feet at the right time, your balance will come automatically. If you get on your feet too late, the nose of your board is likely to go under. When you fall, remember to cover your head with your arms before rising out of the water, since you won't know where your board is or if other surfers are nearby. Once your head is above water, quickly look to see if there are waves or surfers heading your way. When it's all clear, get back on your board, paddle out, and try, try again.

It's Your Turn

Once you're feeling more confident in your ability to catch waves and keep your balance, it's time to turn and ride across the face (front) of the wave. To do this, immediately shift your weight onto your back foot as soon as you stand. Stay low with your knees bent and apply pressure to either your toes or heels of your back foot depending on whether you're riding left or right on the wave. This places pressure on the inside rail of your surfboard. For example, if you are going right on a wave, apply pressure to the right side of the back part of your board. After you've made the turn, release some of the pressure and start cutting across the wave. Keep your eyes trained on the face of the wave as it breaks in front of you (not at the beach or down at your feet). Your body will automatically gravitate toward the direction you look.

Cutting Across

As your surfing confidence and technique improves, cutting across the face of a wave will become easier and easier. The most difficult part for many surfers is pre-determining whether the wave will break to the right or to the left. This takes time, especially if you're surfing a beach break where the waves go in both directions.

In this photo I turned to catch the wave noticing the wave was bigger over my right shoulder making me commit to going left on the wave. Notice my chin is low and I am breathing out as the wave pushes me like other photos to create more glide speed and catch the wave easier.

Here I am looking left as my hands get to the middle of the board to slide up. Also notice my knees and feet close together for tail control of the surfboard as I am being pushed by the wave.

As I feel I have caught the wave I start setting a slight pressure on the left rail/edge of the board. This is usually the next level of your surfing, but it's something you will start thinking about as you improve and want to cut across the face of the wave.

Here again as I slide up to my stance you can see the front knee staying down the middle of the board before twisting my lower body to get my stance.

Now I am up cutting left with my weight over the front foot and will extend my body next for speed in the direction I am looking.

Here I extended which helped me progress faster to the shoulder of the wave or riding the face of the wave. From here is where you become the artist and paint whatever lines, turns and also shows what I believe is your surfing personality.

The best way to determine if a wave is going to break left or right is to recognize which side of the wave is bigger as demonstrated in previous photos. If the wave is coming at you, see if it looks bigger on the left side or right side. I usually tell my students to imagine a line to the horizon. Which side is the wave larger? Once you can determine the larger side, you'll be able to decide which way you'll ride. For example, if I'm paddling for a wave, look over my left shoulder and notice it's bigger on that side, I will try to cut right.

Looking back over your shoulders as you're paddling not only helps you determine the direction the wave is breaking, it allows you to see if another surfer is already up and riding (good etiquette), and lets you know if you're in the right spot to catch the wave. As the wave pushes you, focus your eyes in the direction you'll want to go. At first, beginners have a tendency to look straight down. With practice, you'll notice the type of take off you need and will be inspired by what the wave is doing on what type of path you will want to take.

As you build your knowledge and confidence of how waves break, it's easy to position yourself on the face for the smoothest, best rides. The more time you can spend on the faces of waves, the quicker your flow, style, and ability to learn new tricks will develop.

Chapter 7

Mind Your Manners: Surf Etiquette

Knowing proper surf etiquette is essential to making sure you and everyone near you in the water has fun.

Always remember the person riding the wave closest to the curl has the right of way. If you're using proper paddling technique and looking over your shoulder, you'll be able to see if another surfer has already caught the wave and is heading your way.

If a surfer is already up and riding, pull back and do not go for that wave. Surfers dropping in on one another lead to injuries, damaged boards, and anger. The best surfers know how to anticipate both waves and other surfers. If you're not aware or not very experienced yet, keep away from crowds and other surfers until you're ready.

Try to anticipate what another surfer might do next. Paddling out with other surfers on waves requires familiarity with your own paddling speed, board control and reaction.

If you're paddling out and another surfer is riding a wave toward you, you'll need to think quickly as it is your responsibility to avoid a mishap. You might be able to paddle quickly past the wave, avoiding a collision or forcing the surfer off and ruining his or her ride. If you can't make it past the wave in time, you'll need to go toward the whitewash or already broken part of the wave. It's poor etiquette to get in the way of a surfer riding a wave while you're paddling out. Incidents happen, but try to always hold on to your board. This will help prevent it flying into and injuring any surfers paddling nearby.

Sometimes you'll encounter a local, unfriendly surfer. It's always best to respect the locals. Most have surfed in the same spot for years and rarely enjoy a crowd of unfamiliar faces challenging them for waves. Simply watch, learn and show respect for the locals and other surfers. Most surfers know to share the waves, but others can be quite selfish. If you encounter a "wave hog" simply move away. The ocean is large and there's plenty of room to enjoy waves in another spot without the extra hassle.

I can't stress the importance of surfing away from the crowd until you have the ability to anticipate other surfer's actions and react appropriately. You'll know when you're ready. By using the techniques and tips in this book, you'll have the knowledge you need to practice good surf etiquette and avoid bad situations.

Chapter 8

Conclusion: Surf Safe

I've had many close calls surfing, but the worst have been when it's crowded or the waves are over 6-feet.

There was one winter swell during the late '80s. My friends and I went down to Black's Beach and the waves appeared to have 12- to 15-foot faces. We walked down to Glider Point and noticed they looked even bigger. There were a handful of guys out at two main peaks – the north and south. The swell seemed to be hitting better at the south peak.

We geared up, stretched and waxed our boards. We were on our 6'3" boards because we knew the swell was going to be big.

What we didn't know at the time was larger swell requires larger boards. Otherwise, you'll drop into the wave too late or not have the paddle speed to avoid a bigger set rolling in.

We paddled out using the channel directly south of the peak. When we got out there, we noticed all the other surfer's boards. They had larger boards called "guns." Guns are designed specifically for big waves. They paddle easier and have a narrow outline with a pintail so the rails hold through bottom turns, tube rides, or making the drop.

They're frequently used on the North Shore of Oahu during giant swells.

Between sets, we all started chatting and some of the other surfers told me, "You're going to need a bigger board for these sets." Well, we didn't have bigger boards. We had what we had.

I was there with one old friend who I'd competed with in the past and we always tended to egg one another on.

A set came in and I could see it was the biggest wave we'd ever been in, but the shape was good and peaky. He was in the perfect position. Even though he was closest to the curl (which in surf etiquette gives him the right of way) we both started paddling.

I knew if he didn't go, I would! He pulled back so I went. It was huge! The biggest drop I'd ever taken. I made it and rode the wave a while before cutting out. I was so relieved I didn't wipe out!

When I looked back and saw my friend on the next wave and it was even bigger. He rode screaming past me as I got nailed on the head by a 15-foot wave. The wave pushed me to the bottom and I scrambled, trying to get up. I had nearly reached the surface when I heard a thunderous sound and was pushed back down to the bottom, which felt like a good 10 feet down. I was scared to death and losing oxygen.

As I swam for the surface, yet another wave broke. I was out of air and thinking I would drown. Everyone knows you shouldn't panic, but that's exactly I did. I was underwater and my surfboard was tomb stoning (when the board's nose bobs above water and the other half, attached by leash to the surfer, is shaking back and forth beneath the surface). Finally, by God's grace, I made it up for air and the set was over.

My friend looked at me, asked if I was okay and told me there were no more sets coming. I yelled, "Yes," but I need help getting out of here!"

I was completely out of breath, but going in to shore would be no easy task. I chose to paddle out beyond where the waves were breaking instead and gather my head. After I caught my breath, we continued surfing for another few hours and I rode some of the best waves I've ever had. I can honestly say that day remains the scariest experience I've ever had surfing.

What I know now is I should have ridden the wave closer to shore, got out, and walked back to the channel before attempting to paddle out again. I learned a lot that day. My hope is that this book will help you to avoid some of my mistakes, surf safer, and improve faster.
All of the techniques I've shared in this book have proven to be incredibly helpful to the students I've taught for more than 20 years. I feel confident with

this book, first-time to intermediate surfers can learn the art of surfing and enjoy it for many years.

If after reading this book you're still having difficulty surfing, I'm always available for private lessons. Please visit my site, naturalsurftechnique.com, to learn more.

Happy and safe surfing to you!

-- Frank Caronna
Owner, Natural Surf Technique

Glossary of surfing

Contents
About the Ocean and surfing

About the ocean and surfing

Beach break: *An area where waves are good enough to surf with a beach and sand bottom and waves break on different sand bars*
Blown out: *Where the waves and surf conditions are choppy due to wind-White capped*
Bomb: *A larger set wave than usual*
Close-out: *A wave that doesn't have a rideable direction and breaks all at once with no shape*
Current: *When the ocean is moving from North to south or South to North due to a swell or high wind*
Duck diving: *Paddling through a wave While pushing the nose and tail under the oncoming wave and helps get a surfer out to the waves easier and faster*
Face of wave: *The front of the breaking wave that one would ride across*
Flat: *When the ocean is flat and very small waves or none at all*
Glassy: *When the ocean surface is smooth and not choppy from wind*
Gnarly: *Powerful wave that is usually steep and thick and difficult to ride*
Goofy foot: *When a surfer rides with his/her right foot forward*

Line-up: Where most surfers sit and wait to catch waves that break in the general area they wait for a rideable wave

Outside: The furthest out from the beach where the waves break and are usually the bigger set waves break

Point-break: An area where the waves break off a point sticking out and create longer waves and usually break in only one direction left or right

Rip Tide: An area of water pulling back out to sea and creates an undertow which usually creates a choppy surface or discoloration of water

Reef break: An area where waves break over coral reef or rock area

Regular foot: When a surfer rides with his/her left foot forward

Section: An area of the wave that is surfable for short period and allows a quick tube or maneuver or to be ridden around to get to better part of the wave

Set waves: Larger waves that come in periodically due to a storm or wind activity and are bigger than the average size waves that day

Shoulder: The part of the wave in either direction that has yet broken and allows a longer ride along the face

Snaking: When another surfer drops down a wave in front of another surfer and cuts that surfer off

Swell: A series of waves that travel across the ocean due to a storm and break in shallower water

Tube: *An area of the wave that curls over creating an air pocket and usually more powerful than a wave that crumbles*
Turtle diving/rolling: *When a surfer rolls the board over upside down to get through oncoming waves*
Whitewater: *The foam of the wave after it has broken and pushes toward the beach*

For more info and surf terms go to wikipedia under surf glossary

Printed in Great Britain
by Amazon